STONEMICHAEL ANTONELLI KAROL

The Transfer Of Emotion

The 7 Steps In Sales You Need To Build A Strong Emotional Connection

First published by SMK Media Group 2020

Copyright © 2020 by StoneMichael Antonelli Karol

First edition

ISBN: 9798646134234

Contents

Preface

When you boil it down, selling is about transferring the passion you have for your product or service into the heart of a prospective customer. If you are not succeeding in sales, look at your passion. Passion produces followers. Are people following your advice? If not, you may be lacking passion. Find the true purpose of what you do and what you personally bring to the table.

Transferring passion is similar to a bonfire transferring heat. It's a natural process and draws people to its warmth. Have you lost the passion you once had? If you have lost your original passion perhaps it's time to rediscover what the original motivating factors were and begin to rekindle the fire. When you have passion, you will speak with conviction, act with authority, and present with zeal. If it's lacking, you may have discovered the reason for lack luster performance. Admittedly, there are many neophytes out there who are long on passion, but short on tact or other useful skills thus fumbling good opportunities. Let's face it, **PASSION IS CONTAGIOUS**! There is nothing more contagious than someone who is passionate about a cause, especially if that passion is directed towards an area of need or interest in your life.

In the world of business, nothing moves until it is first sold. It's been said that 90 percent of the decision to buy is made in the heart, the seat of the emotions, and 10 percent of the decision is made in our mind, the seat of the intellect. In fact, it's the intellect that provides logical justification for what the heart is yearning for. If you're going to succeed in sales, you need to be able to speak from the heart to the heart. The fuel, energy, and or language for that communication is passion! Others call it enthus-IASM, the last four letters of which stand for I Am Sold Myself.

So where do we find passion? You must understand the root of passion is emotion. Emotion always precedes passion. Being passionate about something means to be easily moved to strong emotion. What stirs passion in your heart? Does the product or service you represent, stir passion in you? Does the problem your company solves with its product or service, stir emotion in you? If you can't get passionate and enthusiastic about what you have to offer, how can you reasonably expect others to get enthused enough to shell out their hard earned money for it? Perhaps you are passionate about intrinsic things like excellence, value, or service. How does your product or service deliver the values you care deeply about?

Perhaps you sell a type of commodity product such as drill bits. It may be hard to be passionate about drill bits, but you can certainly be passionate about what you personally bring to the table. The level of service you personally will provide, offers insight to the consumer. You can certainly be passionate about gaining mastery in your profession. Selling drill bits may be rather ordinary, but gaining mastery in the art of persuasion and the handling of a wide range of customer dispositions will serve you well your whole life. Be passionate about mastery and the passion you have for the process will quite naturally carry over to your prospect and lead them gently to their best outcome.

Passion changes perspective. Facts inform, but passion moves. Information is static but passion changes the perspective from which something is viewed. If you need to change someone's perspective, inject your passion into the debate and it will most certainly change the dynamic and may well carry the deal.

Whether you have passion or possivity, you can be sure of this, you can only pass on what you have. Make sure it's something worth passing on!

The Relevance of Transferring Emotion In Business

We all have dark moments when we allow our emotions get the better of us, but as soon as the moment passes we start to see things in a different light. Emotions can be powerful drivers in both our personal and our professional lives, but we must learn how to manage them. Otherwise, we are at the mercy of our environment, without having any control over the way we think and act.

But how can we successfully manage our emotions, especially when it comes to business?

There is no situation where emotions aren't in play. The trick is to keep the emotional level in check and make sure you don't see the world through rose-colored glasses (overly optimistic) or blue-colored lenses (overly pessimistic). Basically, an emotion is good; emotion can push you forward. But if your emotions become too extreme (in either a positive or a negative way), it's easy to miss important details.

Learn to check your emotional state. Before each major decision, take a break and clear your head. This could be as simple as taking a walk, drinking a cup of coffee, or a chatting with a friend. During your break, analyze your internal state and create a mental list of the pros and cons of the turmoil you are feeling. If your emotional response lacks balance, you may want to pause before giving an answer or ask a trustworthy third party to give you some advice.

Some studies have shown that emotions triggered by one action (usually anger or frustration) could be transferred to a completely unrelated interaction. To make sure that you don't unleash your anger on an unsuspecting client or possible business partner, it's best to take a step back and understand the source of your emotions before you act on them.

Managing your own emotions can be difficult enough; trying to help others do the same is difficult in an entirely different way. If you feel that the emotions you're seeing from your discussion partner(s) are misdirected, try acknowledging their feelings by saying things like, "I understand this situation can be frustrating" or "I understand this is a real cause for stress and concern in your life." These simple words have the power to defuse a tense situation; most people just want to be heard and understood.

Don't Let Fear of Failure Freeze your Future Break during work

Fear of failure is an incredible, powerful emotion that keeps people in dead-end jobs or positions they don't find attractive. It could also be the thing keeping you from

becoming an entrepreneur, starting a YouTube channel, or traveling the world.

This fear stems from the way we view failure and a fear of the unknown. Back when the only available jobs were for hunters and gatherers, it was logical to fear failure because it helped you survive. However, in today's world, fear of failure can easily be deconstructed by reframing your perspective.

Start by defining the way you see failure and why it makes you anxious, and then redefine the way you see success. Learn to view failure as an opportunity to learn and grow. For instance, a failed product launch can teach you much about how to deal with situations like these in the future and how to recognize that there may be a problem before it's too late.

Another way to defeat the fear of failure is to expand your mindset and learn how to get comfortable with being uncomfortable. The fear may always be by your side, but if you learn to take action in spite of it, you will master the habit of striving for success.

Furthermore, it's crucial to understand that we are living in a dynamic world and you need to stay up to date with the latest technologies and systems in your field or niche. This means that learning never stops. The only way to deal with the fear of failure is to be prepared and outrank your competitors in terms of knowledge.

Use Emotions to Focus on Your Business Goals

Emotions should not deter you from reaching the business goals you set. They should drive you forward. To reach this state of mind, it's crucial to learn how to differentiate between feelings that can be constructive (curiosity, desire for achievement, need for social recognition, and so on) and the ones that are usually destructive (fear, anger, frustration, and more).

The secret to staying focused is to use techniques that tap into your positive emotions and help you get rid of the negative ones. For instance, if you have too many goals on your list, it's easy to feel overwhelmed and frustrated. To avoid feeling this way, trim down your list and only include the goals that must be achieved as quickly as possible. Don't throw away the rest, just put them on a list you'll tackle down the road.

You may also want to break big projects or goals into smaller goals and incremental steps that can be spread out over time. This action reduces the anxiety of working with a task that seems huge and difficult and lets you see that everything is achievable if taken piece by piece.

Finally, don't underestimate the power of breaks. If you find yourself procrastinating or filling your time with jobs that don't really need to be done, take a break. Go for a walk, go to the gym, or have a chat with a friend. Our brains are not designed to constantly be focused on the task at hand, which is why we sometimes need to daydream or disconnect. Allowing ourselves the space and freedom to do this will help us refill our reservoir of energy and motivation.

Whether we like it or not, emotions are an important part of who we are as human beings. They were crucial to our survival in the pre-modern era and can be the perfect business booster in our modern days. To use your emotions to your advantage and learn how to manage them appropriately, you just need to recognize them and your triggers. Developing your ability to self-regulate your emotions will help you stay focused on your goals and allow you to be more successful in business and in life.

1

Chapter One

People Make Decisions Based Off Of Emotion

When it comes to qualifying a prospect it's important to understand the reasons why people purchase, and ultimately, why they will or will not buy your product or service. You see, people will buy to satisfy one of two main needs.

These two needs are:
   The need to avoid pain, or a loss.
   The need to gain pleasure.

These are the two motivating factors in a person for doing anything in their life; to gain pleasure, or to avoid pain. You may have heard it stated this way, "The carrot or the stick". The carrot represents the edible reward, while the stick refers to a punishing switch.
   Your goal in finding the answer to the prospects' problems is to find the pleasure they wish to gain or the pain they wish to avoid, and then show them how your product or service will help them avoid that pain, or gain the pleasure they seek.

Does that make sense?

Great! Let's move on...

People buy products or services based on emotional needs or wants, and then justify their purchase logically. So, in the qualifying phase of the sales process you need to determine the desired results your prospect is seeking. Then you must dig deep to find the prospect's internal (emotional) reasons for wanting to fulfill this want/need.

When you connect with people and understand their emotional reasons for wanting what they desire, you then have tremendous power to give them what they want and have them feel great about buying your product or service. At this point you are probably wondering how to do that.

Let me explain...

In order for a prospect to find value in what you are attempting to sell them, you first must understand they have an issue or situation for which they need some assistance. Once you understand this, you can then show the prospect how your product or service will resolve their issue/situation.

If a prospect doesn't have an issue, or has an issue your product or service will not resolve for them, you'll be spinning your wheels trying to that product/service. Many sales people will attempt to sell their product or service to this prospect; however, it's usually ends poorly for the sales person.

There Are Different Types Of Prospects

As every salesperson knows, every sales negotiation is unique. This means that you must prepare for all potential outcomes. In this industry, you come in contact with many different types of prospects. You have the prospect who knows there is an issue and is eager to find a solution for that issue.

You have the prospect that is somewhat aware that there is an issue; however, the prospect is not quite sure how to go about resolving it. This particular type of prospect may not be aware of any consequences/outcome if the issue remains unresolved. In other, words it's not a priority for them.

The third type of prospect isn't even aware there is a problem. You need to handle each type of prospect in exactly the same way. You need to use the same process of questioning and probing regardless of whether or not the prospect knows there is a problem.

When the prospect shows an obvious need for your product or service, don't fall into the trap many salespeople fall into. Resist the temptation at this point to show them what your product or service will do for them, the benefits of doing business with you and your company, and how much they will invest in what you are selling.

Being too eager can result in the shake of a hand, a thank you for coming, and the prospect deciding to "think about it", and you walk away wondering why you didn't make the sale.

You didn't make the sale because you didn't follow the sales process and proceed with the question and probing phase of the process. You figured you could take a short cut and save yourself some time. What you did was waste your time, and the possibility of making the sale.

Do not, under any circumstances, think you can skip any step, including qualifying. Follow every step in the process. You may think you are saving yourself time, however, in the long run skipping steps will cost you time and money.

So what questions should you ask?

You should always ask open-ended questions. Open-ended questions begin with "who","what", "when", "where", "how" and "why". An open-ended question cannot be answered with "yes or no". Open-ended questions require the prospect to tell you what they think, what they want, or how they feel.

First of all, you want to determine what product or service the prospect is currently using. So, begin with a simple question, "What product or service are you currently using?" Remember, when you ask a question, close your mouth and listen. Don't think about what you are going to say next. Listen to what the prospect is saying, and don't speak until the prospect is finished talking.

An important lesson I have learned in sales is that most people will tell you anything you want to know. All you have to do is ask. People love to talk about themselves, and want to share information about their current situation, problems, likes and dislikes. However, in most cases they need to be prompted. This prompting comes from asking the right questions in the right tone and manner.

When you begin probing, ask general questions. General questions are less threatening; they get the ball rolling, and give you information so you can determine which direction to aim your more specific questions.

Another general question to ask is, "What do you like most about the current product or service you are using?", "What do you like least?", or, "How would you like it to be different?" "If you could design the perfect product or service to meet you needs, what would it do for you?"

The product or service someone currently owns, and what they like or dislike about it, will tell you much about what buying decisions they will make in the future. This line of questioning will give you a general understanding of what they are looking for, and how your product or service fits their needs.

The questions regarding what they like, dislike, or wish were different, will give you some insight into the pain they are looking to avoid, and the pleasure they want to gain. Also, it will tell you if they want something similar to what they currently have, or something different.

You should spend as much time as you need on this phase of questioning. It's important to the process to get as much general information as possible before deciding the direction to take your questioning. Don't be concerned that your prospect will object to the number of questions.

Actually, what you will find, if your questions are asked with a genuine interest and caring attitude, your prospect will be more than willing to share the answers. After all, you're there to help resolve the issue, and if the prospect sees that is really your primary focus, the prospect will relax and tell you anything you want to know.

I know you're thinking you're there to make a sale, and you are; however, as

I've said before, get the dollar signs out of your eyes. "When you stop treating the prospect like a paycheck, and put their needs first, you will be on your way to earning more money than you can imagine".

You need to change your thinking to "How can I provide service?" The compensation you receive is in direct proportion to how much value you provide.

People Feel 7 Powerful Emotions That Drive Their Buying Decisions

1) Fear

Why it matters: Buyers are compelled to speak to salespeople when something's not working the way it should. When a broken process is causing them to miss goals or prevents them from advancing in their career, they'll be afraid that sticking to the status quo won't bode well for them.

How to leverage it in a sale: You should never create a false sense of fear or intimidate your prospects into making a purchase. But in discovery, find out what the prospect stands to lose if things continue as they are, then show how your product will solve these problems — hence taking away their fear.

2) Frustration

Why it matters: People want their lives to be easier and people want to excel at their jobs. When something that's crucial to getting things done is broken, they fail to achieve either of these goals. The frustration they'll feel is a powerful driving force to getting a solution.

How to leverage it in a sale: Ask your buyer why they're talking to you. What's not working today? In their day-to-day, what do they struggle with? What are the ripple effects on the larger organization? The more you let them discuss their gripes, the more open they'll be to hear your solution. This way, your prospects are priming themselves to buy.

3) Hope

Why it matters: Your prospect is frustrated with the status quo, but the flip side of their annoyance is hope that things will get better. You can't just focus on the bad — to close a deal, you have to lead prospects toward their better tomorrow.

How to leverage it in a sale: Ask your prospect, "In your ideal world, how would [process] work? What would you like your day to look like?" This way, you're not only uncovering their goals, you're discovering exactly where their biggest pain points are. You can now tailor your pitch to speak to their hopes for a better future.

4) Excitement

Why it matters: Excitement is imperative for breeding a sense of urgency and keeping the prospect engaged in the sales process. If the prospect becomes bored or disinterested during the conversation, there will be little incentive to continue the conversation.

How to leverage it in a sale: For some prospects, technological innovation and newness will be enough to get them going. Show the prospects demos—Let them get their hands dirty so they stay engaged. For others, hearing about new things they'll be able to accomplish is the key to driving enthusiasm. Figure out what exactly gets your prospect going and play to that.

5) Anger

Why it matters: Anger is one step past frustration. You'll sometimes encounter anger when things have reached a breaking point — a decision needs to be made immediately because a process or tool is so broken that a key project has ground to a halt. You might also see anger rear its head when a prospect who's extremely passionate about your product faces internal blockers.

How to leverage it in a sale: First, acknowledge the anger. You don't want to get your prospect so riled up that the conversation devolves into anger, but recognize that it's there. Then, figure out the source of the anger. If it's coming from the buyer's day-to-day frustrations, determine their top priorities and circle them back to hope. But if they're facing internal resistance or other blockers, channel their emotion into something productive and help them sell your tool to the economic buyer.

6) Fear of missing out (FOMO)

Why it matters: Fear of missing out is a very specific subset of general fear. It's not always an individual fear of Prospects don't want to be the ones who are responsible for their company missing out on the next big thing or getting left behind by their competition.

How to leverage it in a sale: Show your prospects case studies of customers similar to themselves who have seen success with your product. Circulate third-party research that demonstrates that your proposed business plan/product solves is not just a trend — explain how not addressing the situation, not moving quickly, will result in leaving your prospect leagues behind the industry.

7) Desire to be first

Why it matters: This is a simple issue of business acumen. Every company needs a comparative advantage to survive, much less flourish, and successful businesspeople (whether or not they're entrepreneurs) usually have a competitive drive fueling them.

How to leverage it in a sale: Appeal to your prospect's competitive nature by explaining benefits in a way that highlights exactly the business advantages this will provide them.

What Are You Really Selling?

Here are some strong motivators that drive people to sell along with some traditional B2B examples.

1. Affluence/Status

It is important for some people to have others know that they have money. It provides validation that they are doing well— high status and makes them feel good about themselves. This plays directly with motivation. Look how many people buy Apple computers or Tesla cars, classy brand names known to be more expensive.

A good application of this in B2B sales is selling a premium version of your product, like LinkedIn Premium. Now you get a premium member badge next to your profile. Or you could pay hundreds of thousands of dollars to be a

Diamond level sponsor of Dreamforce, with maximum exposure on marketing material and prime real estate at the conference.

Here is how you can use affluence/status to sell:

Focus on the personal benefits.

How can the results a prospect will get make a good impression on his/her boss? How can it help him/her move up in their career faster?

Highlight the specific ROI.

What is the monetary return your prospect will see, and how can you make sure all decision makers and stakeholders are aware?

Use anecdotes to make it real for your prospects.

Do you have any case studies that demonstrate the exact benefit your prospect is looking for? Even better, do you have any customers who received a promotion after using your product and who are willing to talk to prospects? Using words like reward, valuable, exclusive, distinguishing, profitable, and gaincan help you paint the picture.

2. Reassurance

Peace of mind is priceless in playing to the power motivation. People want to have control over their lives. You can't put a price on feeling safe and protected. This is the business at which insurance salespeople and financial planners make a living.

When it comes to B2B sales, reassurance could mean buying a well known and highly integrated customer management platform, like Salesforce. Smaller and less known solutions may be cheaper, but Salesforce is a known and trusted brand. You know what you are getting, and there are no hidden costs or surprises. This is highly effective when trust in a category of products in general is low.

Here's how you can use reassurance to sell:

· Describe what your product will do for the prospect. Will this allow the prospect to stop worrying about this one thing and focus on more important things in their business?

- Use any sign(s) of trust to your advantage. Have you received any awards or recognition in your industry? Do you have any additional training or certifications that will put your prospect more at ease?
- Share knowledge and statistics with your prospects. Do you have any industry reports or white papers that show tangible results? Do you have any case studies of users just like them that are seeing the desired results?
- Prove others have already put their trust you. Do you have any recognizable companies already using your product? Do you have any testimonials from high-level individuals?
- Capitalizing on emotional words like guarantee, results, improve, satisfaction, a leader in, secure, safe, trusted and reliable can help you win trust.

3. Time/Convenience

This plays to an individual's needs for achievement. If your customer is a working professional, busy parent, or anyone else with extremely limited time or energy, then selling convenience is a piece of cake. Thus, the On-Demand economy is born. Traditional examples range from housekeeping services to drive-throughs to dog walkers.

This is a particularly hot space right now for tech. You can find nearly everything on-demand. SaaS companies, sometimes referred to as "on-demand software," are taking advantage of our increasing need to have things right away. Great examples are Datanyze and Lead411 to get sales leads immediately. Companies like Hired or CloserIQ are great for finding sales talent for your company.

Here's how can you use time/convenience to sell:

- Translate the value for them in terms of time lost. How much time are they losing by continuing to do things the way they are? What are the long-term consequences if they don't do take action now?

- Remind your prospect how much energy their current solution is costing them. What are the other areas that are being affected? How is your solution vastly superior?
- Help them realize what else they could/should be doing. What would they rather be doing? What are the more important things that could be done with their time? How much more effective would they be at their job if they could get this one area under control?
- Using words like productivity, effectiveness, simple, quick, "plug and play", and "done for you" will help them realize how much time they could be saving.

4. Pleasure

We all have this particular weak spot: We will pay almost any amount to enjoy a little more pleasure in our lives. For me, my guilty pleasure is — you probably guessed it already — coffee! You with me? I'd gladly pay $8+ for the perfectly brewed cup. But every one has something, whether it's sports cars, luxury vacations, massages, gourmet food, etc.

Though B2B selling isn't usually about selling pleasure, many companies buy products for the office that give them pleasure. For example, how many companies have expensive coffee makers and machines in their offices to keep employees happy and energized?

Here's how can you use pleasure to sell:

- Translate the value of pleasure for your prospect. How does your product ultimately help your prospect become happier, whether it's a direct impact or indirect? How does your product provide value?
- Make using your product enjoyable. How can you make the experience of using your product as enjoyable as possible? How can you surprise and delight your prospects?
- Help the prospect imagine a brighter future. How can you paint the picture of a more desirable future? What would the ideal scenario be for the prospect?

- Choosing words such as fun, please, imagine, enjoy, satisfy, you, delight and opportunity play to the pleasure emotions.

5. Personal Empowerment

The whole self-improvement industry is one of the most lucrative industries of all time. Power is the main driver of motivation in this category. Americans are spending over $11 billion per year, and it continues to rise. Every human has dreams and aspirations. If you can help them become a better person and reach their dreams, you've hit the jackpot. This includes everything from fitness to finance to emotional health, and so much more.

Some of my favorite tech examples of this are subscription services like Harvard Business Review and AA-ISP. Events are a big source of revenue for companies that are selling knowledge and networking, such as Sales Stack, SaaStr and Dreamforce.

Here is how you can use personal empowerment to sell:

- Proudly present and publicize awards and recognition your customers have received. Have any of your customers made headlines after utilizing your product? Do you have pictures of your customer receiving their accolades?
- Offer to highlight your prospect if they go with you. Does your prospect need publicity that you can offer? Would they make a good case study?
- Choosing words like image, respect, powerful, reputation, prominence, influence and prestige are sure to evoke emotions.

2

Chapter Two

Qualifying Your Potential Customer

One of the main roles of a support team is to field customer questions and concerns. And while many of your customers will bring their issues to your attention through your support channels, some of them will not. Instead, they'll become frustrated when trying to deal with an issue on their own or simply switch to one of your competitors — neither of which is good for your business.

So instead of fully relying on your customers to alert you to their struggles, it's in your best interest to take a proactive approach to identify and address them.

Why You Should Actively Look for Customer Issues

If you don't yet have a strategy for identifying your customers' issues, it might sound a bit counterintuitive. After all, your customer service team likely already has plenty to do, and each issue you uncover means more work for them. Plus, customers who are really struggling will let you know. Right? Not necessarily.

In fact, one study found that only 1 in 26 unhappy customers will take the time to complain. The remaining 25 will "churn" and stop dealing with your company.

So if you're not yet taking a proactive approach to finding problems, you're missing the opportunity to address your customers' needs before they leave your company altogether. On the upside, this means that taking steps towards identifying customer struggles could make a MAJOR impact on your retention rates. It could be exactly what you need to achieve the kind of growth you want.

Ways to Identify Your Customers' Issues and Concerns

Deciding that you want to be more proactive about addressing your customers' problems is easy. Knowing where to begin is a little more challenging. But with the following four steps, you can work toward creating a strategy that works for your business and enables you to address each of your customers' needs more effectively.

1. Send Surveys Regularly

The most straightforward method for identifying your customers' struggles is simply asking. And the easiest way to do that is with customer surveys. Of course, this strategy isn't exactly groundbreaking.

Surveys were one of the earliest methods of collecting customer feedback, even before online platforms simplified the process and eliminated the need for pen-and-paper responses. And despite the many advances that make it easy for businesses to collect data, surveys are still one of the most popular options.

In fact, if you currently have any method in place for learning about your customers, this is likely it. But there are a few reasons why customer surveys are the go-to approach for many businesses. They're easy to create, they work well with automation, and they can provide a ton of valuable insight.

If you're not yet sending surveys on a regular basis, this is a great starting point for evaluating how well you're meeting your customers' needs.

Plus, your surveys don't need to be complex to be helpful. Even a basic CSAT survey can be a solid starting point for gauging overall satisfaction with your brand. Then, once you've established a basic setup for your surveys, you can start sending more advanced versions.

And though the questions you ask depend on your industry, business model, and brand, it's a good idea to include at least a few that allow for open-ended responses. This way, your customers can voice concerns that you may not yet be aware of. And if you notice any recurring trends or patterns in their answers, this is a clear indicator of where your business has room for improvement.

2. Save and Organize Feedback

Regardless of the exact methods you use to collect customer feedback, it's essential to have a straightforward method in place for saving and organizing it. After all, collecting survey data and other feedback is only helpful if you put it to use. Having it all in one logical, organized place will make the entire process much easier.

So if you haven't yet done so, implement a system for collecting feedback. Depending on the platform you use to create surveys, you may not have to take any additional steps to do this. With Freshdesk's CSAT surveys, for example, users automatically have access to a response dashboard. But regardless of how the platform you use displays results, it's essential to organize your data in a way that makes sense to you and your team.

It's also worth noting that most survey platforms today offer users the ability to download results as CSV or XLS files. So if you prefer to save your data in spreadsheet form, this is an easy option.

Then, once you've created an organizational method that works for your team, you can analyze your results with a focus on identifying common themes. And, while it's possible to draw helpful conclusions from any type of question, you'll want to pay special attention to the information your customers provided in open-ended forms.

In most cases, this is where you'll uncover specific problems, complaints, and suggestions. If you notice any pieces of feedback that appear in multiple surveys, focus on addressing those points first.

After all, for every customer that takes the time to complete your survey and tell you about a problem, there's likely another dozen dealing with the same issue. Coming up with a solution could have a major impact on your overall customer satisfaction.

3. Aim to Understand Confusion

Some of your customers (and prospective customers) will reach out for clarification when they're confused about some aspect of your products or services. And in many cases, all it takes to eliminate their confusion is a sentence-long explanation.

But for each of these customers who reach out with a question, it's safe to assume that there is at least a handful of others that are having trouble understanding the same thing. For example, let's say that a customer is frustrated because they misunderstood your pricing information and are now facing costs that are higher than expected.

The easy solution here would be to apologize for the misunderstanding, explain their invoice, and offer to adjust it. And while that might be enough for this particular customer, it's important to consider that others may have run into the same issue.

So instead of looking at their situation as a unique misunderstanding, take the time to understand what caused the confusion and look at ways to adjust your pricing information to make it more straightforward. After all, if other customers run into the same problem, they might simply get frustrated and stop working with your company altogether.

If a simple conversation and a few tweaks to your site copy can prevent this from happening even once, it's entirely worth your time.

4. Let Customers Provide Feedback on Your Site

The easier you make it for customers to provide feedback, the more likely they will be to give you the kind of helpful insight you're looking for. And while surveys are a great start, today there are a variety of ways to make it even more convenient for your customers to provide feedback.

For example, today many sites use feedback widgets which allow visitors to share problems, concerns, and issues as they browse. With this approach, visitors don't even need to navigate to a contact page or write an email to have their opinions heard.

Making a process of collecting feedback convenient for your customers will allow you to be even more effective at identifying their struggles and addressing them before they negatively impact your business.

Create High Value To Make Power Sales

If you are going to deliver high value to your customers, the first thing you need to address is how to resolve their problems.

What Problems Do You Solve for Your Customers?

Sales is about solving customer problems/issues, whether the issues/problems are current, or situations they will face as their marketplace evolves and their needs change. When I asked a top sales professional about what he did that allowed him to stand out in his field, he responded very simply, "I solve problems." Simple, but not easy!

If you can't put your finger on your customer's problem, you won't be able to resolve it. Worse, you will waste time and lose credibility. You must be able to understand the issue clearly from the customer's point of view. and describe a solution clearly so that the customer sees its value. To find out what the really difficult problems are, ask the right questions and listen before acting.

The overarching challenge, or goal, for most executives is how to make their businesses more profitable, as quickly, reliably, and as inexpensively as possible, so they can be assured that they will remain in business, keep the owners happy, and keep their jobs. These other problems are related to that main concern; for example,

- Finding new customers
- Keeping existing customers
- Selling more to existing customers
- Improving customer service
- Reducing personnel costs
- Reducing customer complaints
- Decreasing time to market
- Improving market share (or mind share)
- Taking advantage of new technology
- Improving morale
- Developing new products
- Leaving markets or closing units

The most successful salespeople are the ones who identify pressing customer issues and do something to resolve them in a way that is convenient, cost effective, or timely. Top salespeople identify problems that customers are ready to solve, then they work hard to resolve them. Of course, identifying problems and then delivering good solutions for them requires a well-planned and organized effort. This book provides the steps for delivering high-value, innovative customer solutions and recommendations for identifying the customer's priorities for solving those problems.

Top sales professionals know that when you find customers' significant, pressing problems, they will be willing to pay for a solution. Finding those significant problems means sorting out customers who are ready and willing to buy from those who are not. A critical success factor is how to market your problem-solving abilities so people know what you can do for them and how that they can save time, money or effort by using your solutions.

Taking the initiative to identify and decide to solve customer-related problems in unique ways is leadership. Sales leaders open untapped and sometimes vast new market opportunities. What issues are you solving for your customers? If you were to ask your customers, what would they say? If you asked them to prioritize those challenges, would there be any surprises? Identify the issues that your customers want to solve the most and that you are most uniquely qualified to resolve and you will have a winning combination. So, how do you solve problems? There are proven problem-solving steps you can use. You may use them already. Let's take a look at one approach.

Five Step Problem-Solving Approach

People who are really good at solving problems go about it systematically. They have a way of placing the problem in context. They don't jump to conclusions. They evaluate alternatives. A good way to become a systematic problem solver is to adopt the following five-step problem-solving process:

Identify the problem

This is critical, you must try to solve the right problem. Don't try to solve a problem the customer sees as low priority or unimportant. Identify the right problem by asking the right questions and observing. You cannot identify the customer's problems by presenting your products. What's leading the customer to feel there is a problem? Is it something specific or is it an intuitive sense that things aren't as they should be? Can the customer define the problem?

Analyze the problem

How severe is the problem? How often does it occur? Are there any special circumstances that are present when it occurs? What might be the cause(s) of the problem? Can you rule out any causes? How long has it been going on? Has it gotten worse? How is the problem affecting other processes or people?

Identify decision criteria

How will you and the customer make decisions when it is time to decide? How will you weigh the criteria? Can you identify independent standards that can be used?

Develop multiple solutions

Do not stop at the first solution that you or others identify. It may be good, but much better ones may exist. Evaluate alternative scenarios. As objectively as possible, assess the pros and cons of each.

Choose the optimal solution

Use the criteria you developed in the third step of this problem-solving process to choose the best solution. Develop a base of support that will ensure you can implement the solution. Prepare for contingencies.

When you solve problems systematically, you save time, achieve better solutions, and increase your credibility with the customer and the perceived value of what you've done. If you can solve problems the customer is facing more expeditiously than someone else, the customer will appreciate the time saved.

Problem-solving involves some considerations beyond those addressed by the five-step process. Once you have the problem identified, you can sometimes rely on a known solution or a combination of known solutions. At other times, no ready solution is apparent. In this case, you may need to do a business case analysis to determine if it will be profitable for your company to develop a solution. This includes asking what might be involved in developing the solution, how much time the process would require, and how well suited your company is to do the job. The issues become more complicated, but the problem-solving process may also be more rewarding.

You may need to tap into the knowledge you have acquired in solving similar or even non-similar problems or the knowledge that exists in your company. You may need to have someone initiate research and create a solution from scratch, (which can be cost prohibitive), or you can find a partner that already has the solution you need. You will need an innovative approach. Deciding to create solutions and driving them through the organization is part of what makes exceptional sales leaders exceptional.

3

Chapter Three

It's Not About What They Want, It's About What They Need

What is Buyer Motivation?

Buyer motivation is the set of psychological factors behind a consumer's decision to make a particular purchase. That purchase is the end result of a process referred to as the "Buyer's Journey" — a three-stage process consisting of:

- Awareness.
- Consideration.
- Decision.

Some may define this using a different number of stages, but the underlying concepts are the same. Let's take a look at these stages and examine how they relate to a buyer's purchasing motivation.

Awareness

This is the primary stage of the journey, where a buyer becomes aware of a problem, want, or need. It could be the need to purchase a smoke detector, or renter's insurance, or anything for that matter. The motivation here can be either internal or external (we will go into further detail about the differences in the next section), and it's important that pain-points be addressed to help identify the problem.

Consideration

Once a buyer is aware of their problem (or want or need), they are then motivated to start gathering information. At this stage buyers are considering their options, so providing any product education resources like product specs, reviews, and other details will be greatly appreciated.

Decision

It's at this stage where the buyer is motivated to make a final decision and has determined that their needs have been met. One important note to keep in mind stems from a 2009 study which discovered that two factors can affect final purchasing decisions:

- Negative feedback from other customers
- The level of motivation to comply or accept the feedback

The study's authors noted the following example for a customer at the decision stage:

A customer chooses to buy a Nikon D80DSLR camera. However, because his good friend, who is also a photographer, gives him negative feedback, he will then be bound to change his preference. Motivation itself can be generated either internally or externally – psychologists refer to this as intrinsic versus extrinsic motivation.

Internal motivation is what drives us to make decisions based on our own wants and/or needs. It steers our behavior and actions toward goals and outcomes that are personally rewarding to us.

A consumer may have a desire — a want — to purchase a new car that's more luxurious than their current model. By the same token, that same consumer may also be driven by the need to replace an older vehicle in decline.

External motivation, on the other hand, is driven by outside factors in our environment. This is either the desire to gain something or avoid/mitigate risk and can be based upon rules and regulations or social pressure. While bike helmets are required by law in some places, even in the absence of legal consequences there is a fear of looking reckless in front of peers.

Coming back to the smoke detector reference from earlier, there can be multiple motives based on a buyer's persona. Homeowners, landlords, and renters are motivated in different ways in terms of why they purchase one — whether fear of code violations, fines, evictions, or lawsuits.

How to Determine Your Seller Motivation

Before we dive deeper into the motivations of our customers, it's important to begin with a degree of self-examination and reflect on what your own motivations are as a seller. The questions below will help to guide you in gaining more insight into your customer's decision-making process.

Where do you want your product to be positioned in the market?

Seller, know thyself! Where — and what — do you want to be? Some auto manufacturers such as Lamborghini or Aston Martin, consider themselves to be firmly placed in the high-end luxury market. Others, such as Hyundai, offer models appealing to different price points, with the Accent, Elantra, and Sonata lines. For home furniture retailers, you have Walmart positioned on one end and Ethan Allen on the other (with IKEA sitting somewhere in the middle).

Who do you want to sell to?

Who do you want your customers to be? Are they utilitarian, looking for only basic features/functions to accomplish the task, or status and prestige-driven, desiring extras that will make the experience even better? Are they budget conscious, or is cost not an object?

- What is your definition of a successful customer?
- What is a happy customer to you?

Is it someone who will write glowing product reviews on your site or elsewhere on social media? What factors do you deem most important that will drive repeat business? Figure these out for your customer base and you will have a much better insight into both your motivations as well as theirs.

How to Segment Customers Based on Motive

An assortment of of factors can influence our decision to purchase a particular product. It could be the need to signal prestige to impress our peers (or ourselves), or it could be the need to address a concern regarding physical safety, money, loss of time, or simply what many millennials call "FOMO" (Fear Of Missing Out).

Now let's think about shoes for a moment.

If you're a nurse or restaurant worker, you will probably be more interested in something best suited to handle being on your feet all day. If you work in an industrial setting, comfort is also going to be important, but the safety provided by a pair of steel-toe boots with non-skid soles will take precedence. For those who favor form over function, it might be the right pair of Allen Edmonds oxfords or Manolo Blahnik pumps.

And what about aspirational buyers?

While professional athletes, like LeBron James or Kevin Durant, wear Nike's high-performance sneakers on the court, plenty of customers who never see the inside of a basketball court are still inspired to pay $200 or more to have the same footwear as their idols (Saturday Night Live made a hilarious fake commercial about this back in 2013).

An extremely helpful method that you can apply in terms of buyer motivation comes from the VALS Framework, used by marketers for decades now. Consumers are segmented into one of eight different types, based on psychological and demographic traits along two dimensions: resources available and primary motivations. These primary motivators are ideals, achievement, and self-expression.

The eight VALS types are as follows:

- Innovators
- Thinkers
- Believers
- Achievers
- Strivers
- Experiencers
- Makers
- Survivors

When determining messaging, many of our clients have asked us to help segment their customers, whether newly acquired or long established. Leveraging machine learning and advanced analytics can help identify the most relevant attributes relating to demographics, psychographics, geography, and behavior, which can help inform buyer personas alongside VALS types.

Translating Motives Into Ecommerce Action

We've examined the psychology behind what drives consumers to make a purchase decision while reflecting inward to understand what your own motives are as a seller and how you view yourself in the market place.

Drilling down further, we explored how to best segment your customers based on the different motivations. With our discussions around theory out of the way, let's get more practical now and figure out how you can translate this into action and market to buyer motives. The key take-away here is that motive needs to drive site design. When we talk about site design, there are three primary factors we need to consider — all of which play a crucial role in successful customer engagement.

User interface

User interface (UI) deals with the look and feel of a site. The psychological influences behind the choice of color have long been understood by designers. We know that red can invoke feelings of passion, while blue can help calm us. This also applies to font choice — sans serif fonts can look more modern, while serif fonts have a more traditional appearance — as well as the images you place on your site.

If you're selling a hammer designed to break through a car window in an emergency, you need to appeal to your customer's sense of fear and need for safety. Bold fonts, shades of red, and the right images will invoke these senses to motivate them toward purchasing your your product.

Conversely, if you're selling high-end perfumes, you need to appeal to your customer's sense of prestige and luxury. Images of attractive and glamorous people subconsciously motivate your customers to want to aspire to be them.

User experience

The user experience (UX), in contrast to the user interface, describes the navigation of your site. This ties into how you group your products and present your categories, and what filters and facets you use to help customers narrow down their choices.

Customer motivation should drive the user experience — a fashion buyer looking for dress shoes, for instance, will be more interested in filtering by color than something like durability, whereas the opposite may apply to someone looking for work shoes for a factory setting (safety- motivated vs. prestige).

Non-catalog content

This can include blogs, product reviews, or videos. Anything that you put on your site for your customers' consumption needs to be able to reflect your brand and speak to their motivations. Having a blog alongside your content, not only helps with SEO — it also is a great hub for shoppers who are interested in learning more about your product or your industry.

Having product reviews (bonus points if they include pictures) helps users understand the pros and cons of each product, and can even help to answer any lingering questions they may have.

Videos of people interacting with, using, or wearing your product helps put dimensions into context, and add an additional resource for shoppers who are wondering what the physical product looks like.

Ways to Look for Buyer Motives

Armed with this clearer understanding of your customers' motivations and how to put that into action as a seller, the final piece of the puzzle is to know what signals to watch for. Here are four ways to look for your buyer's motives:

What are customers asking your customer service reps?

Leverage the wealth of information that comes from the conversations your service reps are having with your customers. Are they asking for guarantees, discounts, refunds? Find out what they are asking questions about, as well as what they are asking for — examine those trends over both the short and long-term to gain better insight.

What specific categories or products are buyers looking at on your site?

Alongside gleaning important details from your service rep's conversations, tracking your buyer's activities is crucial. Being as familiar as possible with what your buyers are looking at (and where) on your site will allow you to have a far more detailed understanding of their motivations.

Use marketing mix analytics to determine which channels work the best

Employing predictive analytics can enable sellers to analyze their marketing allocation. Understand the impact of their marketing efforts, and how to determine the optimal mix and budget to maximize ROI. Companies that use marketing mix analytics tend to drive an average of 40% improvement in marketing campaigns, while also being better able to balance short-term marketing and promotion tactics with long-term brand building needs.

Use web analytics to determine any geographic and/or psychographic segments

Google Analytics provides a wealth of information about your customers. Consider the Behavior Flow report, which will allow you to see how visitors are interacting with your site. Site analytics will allow you to uncover insights about your customer base. You might encounter geographic and/or personality segments you may have never thought to market to before!

Executive Summary

Buyer motivation is the driving force behind what makes your customers decide to make purchases on your site.

Engaging with them at whichever stage they are at in their journey, knowing the right psychological factors at play, and being able to know yourself and how to correctly position your products in the market place complete this picture. Armed with this insight, you can properly segment your customers based on their individual motives, whether those be fear, safety, pleasure, or prestige.

Leveraging this knowledge by tailoring your site's aesthetics, navigation, and supplemental content, and understanding what signals to look for as your customers interact with you can turn insight into action.

Customers are motivated by achievement

While it might not be as powerful as joy, the desire to achieve is another incredibly strong motivator to get customers invested in your brand. We all know the pride of having completed a project or overcome an obstacle, and that drive to reach a goal can be exactly what your customer is looking for.

Motivate your customers with emotion, not advertisements

Your brand is worth getting to know, but only if you position it properly. If you're relying on advertisements to encourage customers to explore your store, you've made your business into a vending machine that nobody is going to have time for.

However, if you take care to look at the things that really motivate your customers — like their desire for belonging, the positive effects of joy, and the pride of achievement — you can start building a brand community that not only forms emotional relationships with customers but also gets new ones interested, keeping every one engaged for a long, long time.

What Motivates Customers to Buy?

Understanding the psychology behind what makes customers want to buy is important in helping to improve your sales figures. If you are able to tap into the motivation behind purchases you can tailor your marketing better and improve your chance of increasing conversion rates. Here are five motivations you can use to convince customers to buy products or services from your small business:

They need your product

The first motivation is convincing your potential customers that they don't just want your product, but that they need it. If your customer is currently dissatisfied, they may be looking for a way to right a wrong. Your aim is to convince customers that your product or service will make that wrong a right.

One way you can do this is to distinguish between a feature and a benefit. This can be done through the language. Avoid using general statements. Say "our customers report an average 30% decrease in costs, about twice the industry average when using our products" rather than "our product makes you more productive." You should also be aware that the greater the dissatisfaction, the higher the urgency a customer will feel.

Your product will make their life easier

We live in a time where convenience is highly valued. Why do you think fast food and microwavable meals have become so popular? By using this motivation you can convince customers that your product will make their lives easier, will save them time or will save them money. Some companies market their products by indicating how quickly the customer recovers the spend purchase. Highlight how simple your returns policy is or how much time previous customers have saved using your product.

Fear & Safety

If your customer is scared of something, for example their safety, they may be more likely to purchase your products and services to prevent any bad eventualities. Fear is often used in advertising and works well at engagement.

By using shocking images or statistics, you can stir a feeling of fear in your customers. The car industry does this particularly well, often highlighting safety features and how such features can protect loved ones, however the technique used in a range of industries from security (alarms and locks) to beauty (SPF preventing sun cream, anti-wrinkle creams preventing aging).

Convenience

To use this motivation you need to show how convenient your brand is. For example if you run a dental practice late night or weekend appointments provide this convenience. Your method of delivery, physical location, or simply the ease of use of your website can all contribute to this motivation. If the shopping experience is straightforward this will motivate customers to buy, and even to come back to purchase again.

Exclusiveness

Customers like to feel as though they are special and by offering exclusivity within your product offering you will help to ignite this feeling. You can do this in a number of ways - perhaps through offering an exclusive discount via email marketing to certain customers, or through selling an item made in limited numbers, or which is custom-made.

4

Chapter Four

Making Your Customer Sell Themselves

Poor economic growth has caused many businesses to reevaluate the strength of their partnerships. As a result, vendors and suppliers that do not perform well are increasingly put on the chopping block. This trend doesn't bode well given how many vendors are able to provide what customers are looking for. According to Gallup's "Guide to Customer Centricity: Analytics and Advice for B2B Leaders," only 31 percent of businesses believe their suppliers understand their needs.

If you plan on seeking a high-level leadership role in business, you'll need to acknowledge how an effective sales pitch mitigates this customer-supplier issue (the pitch isn't just a chance to show off your product). In today's business climate, your pitch must convince potential customers that you recognize their struggles and understand their concerns. By supporting the vendor-client relationship in such a positive manner, you reduce your risk of churn. This is true of any endeavor, whether you're a startup entrepreneur trying to get investors or a manager of sales trying to re-engage a high-profile client.

That said, business operations have changed in such a way that old pitching techniques such as lengthy slide decks and requesting non-disclosure agreements—no longer work.

The sales leaders of today and tomorrow need to adapt accordingly.

Ways to perfect your sales pitch to any audience

Know the Modern Buyer

Clients are more likely to research a product or vendor long before getting in contact with sales. They pore through product descriptions, read consumer reviews, and search trade publications for additional insight. Businesses have adapted accordingly, creating free assets like white papers and case studies to display their expertise. As such, with so much information available, prospective clients in the initial stages of their buyer's journeys have higher levels of knowledge regarding a particular service than in years past.

Unfortunately, many sales teams haven't kept up. They still focus on preliminary talking points, restating information that clients have already learned. While the prospect's questions now are more specific and in depth, and thus, some salespeople are unprepared to answer them.

Understanding modern client actions and motivations ahead of time can help you avoid such scenarios. As a salesperson, you need a thorough grasp of your products and services and must anticipate unusual or hypothetical questions. Similarly, as Gallup's research indicated, you need an intimate understanding of the client's needs. Just as potential customers or investors research your business, so too should you research theirs. Below are 3 tips for doing so:

- See what assets they have available, then think critically about what sort of services they need to sell their products or why your portfolio or business philosophy makes for a good investment.
- Identify pain points within the industry, both common and uncommon. Get as specific as possible. The more you understand about what the prospect needs and how he or she finds solutions, the better equipped you are to create a convincing sales pitch.

· Research prospects when crafting your pitch.

Understand the Prospect's Risk Tolerance

Steve W. Martin, the founder of the Heavy Hitter Sales training program, noted that risk tolerance changes depending on the department. He commented that an information technology manager is more willing to gamble on a vendor than a marketing manager might be, meaning these two individuals will view the same sales pitch with different attitudes. Whereas marketing may be more willing to take a chance, IT will demand more examples, specifications, case studies, and other elements of proof before entering a partnership. After surveying over 230 business professionals, Martin provided a chart that provides a brief look at the risk- tolerance percentages of different departments. A higher tolerance means the department is more willing to risk losing money to get better results.

Enhance Your Communication

Effective communication is essential for sales. Instead of talking at a potential client or investor, modern sales techniques require you to hold a reciprocal conversation. Doing so demonstrates you respect prospects and understand their needs, which can help them view your business more favorably. Similarly, listening to investors and answering their questions in a trustworthy manner shows your commitment to their interests, not just your own.

Communication puts your soft skills on full display, but many graduates are deficient in this area. According to a Payscale survey, only 46 percent of graduates are effective communicators. This is why you should focus on developing your soft skills. Practice active listening and try viewing projects from another person's point of view. Furthermore, if you choose to work while getting your degree, you can get real-world experience by practicing your soft skills while on the job.

Focus on Collaboration

Sales is typically seen as a single-person undertaking, despite the fact that the outcome of a pitch affects the whole company. By thinking of sales as a collaborative activity, you can bring new perspectives into your pitch and may find points for improvement you wouldn't have seen otherwise. Even if you attend meetings alone, developing your pitch with other people helps ensure success.

Learn to Communicate with the C-suite

Salespeople are used to talking to people in mid-level and upper management, but their skills may not be ready for executive-level prospects. According to Martin, only 31 percent of salespeople are effective at communicating with senior executives. This shortfall is unfortunate, as these business leaders are often the decision makers. You can't land the sale without them, even if you successfully pitch to management.

The difference between talking to managers and executives lies in their distinct points of view. Managers are concerned with their teams' efficiency, while executives are focused on the business as a whole. When pitching to the C-suite, explain how your service reduces overall operating costs, minimizes friction in production, offers other such benefits that have an impact company-wide. Reading trade news and publications is also beneficial, as doing so helps you recognize which industry issues are currently at the top of executives' minds.

Strengthen Your Close

Even a perfect pitch can come apart at the close. Instead of using this moment to secure a sale, take time to remind potential clients why partnering with your company is beneficial. Prompt them by asking if they see the potential for a partnership, and if they say yes, ask why. Having the client verbally express this viewpoint solidifies the idea that working with you or your company is a good decision.

Furthermore, when the prospect or investor accepts your pitch, it's time to stop pushing. You've achieved your initial goal, so now you must deliver what you promised. It is best to save upsells for later in the relationship when the client has developed trust.

Direct Marketing

Direct marketing is an advertising strategy that relies on the individual distribution of a sales pitch to potential customers. Mail, email, and texting are among the delivery systems used. It is called direct marketing because it generally eliminates the middleman such as advertising media.

How Direct Marketing Works

Unlike most marketing campaigns, direct marketing campaigns do not rely on advertising in mass media. Instead, they deliver their sales pitches by mail, by phone, or by email. Although the number of pitches sent can be massive, an attempt is often made to personalize the message, by inserting the recipient's name or city in a prominent place.

The call to action is a common factor in much of direct marketing. The recipient of the message is urged to immediately respond by calling a toll-free phone number, sending in a reply card, or clicking on a link in an email promotion. Any response is a positive indicator of a prospective purchaser. This variety of direct marketing is often called direct response marketing.

Targeting in Direct Marketing

The most effective direct marketing campaigns use lists of targeted prospects in order to send their messages only to the likeliest prospects. The lists might target families who have recently had a baby, or new homeowners, or recent retirees with products or services that they are most likely to need.

Catalogs are a form of direct marketing with a history that dates back to the latter half of the 19th century. In modern times, catalogs are usually sent only to consumers who have indicated an interest in a previous purchase of a similar product.

The Advantages and Disadvantages of Direct Marketing

A direct marketing pitch that is delivered to the widest possible audience is probably the least effective. That is, the company may gain a few customers while merely annoying all of the other recipients. Junk mail, spam email, and texting all are forms of direct marketing that many people can't get rid of fast enough.

Many companies engage in opt-in or permission marketing, which limits their mailing or emailing to people who have indicated a willingness to receive it. Having lists of opted-in subscribers can be particularly valuable as they indicate a real interest in the products or services being advertised.

Who Uses Direct Marketing

Despite its drawbacks, direct marketing has its appeal, particularly to companies on a shoestring budget who can't afford to pay for television or internet advertising campaigns.

Direct marketing is the preferred advertising strategy for small local businesses, which can distribute hundreds of flyers, coupons, or menus for less than it would cost them to place an ad or make a commercial.

By its nature, the effectiveness of a direct marketing campaign is easier to measure than other types of advertising. This is because they often contain a call to action. The company an measure its success by how many consumers make the call, return the card, use the coupon, or click on the link.

- Direct marketing relies on distribution to individual consumers rather than advertising in mass media.
- The call to action is a common factor in much of direct marketing.
- The effectiveness of direct marketing is easier to measure compared to media advertising.

Definition of 'Personal Selling'

Personal selling is also known as face-to-face selling in which one person who is the salesman tries to convince the customer in buying a product. It is a promotional method by which the salesperson uses his or her skills and abilities in an attempt to make a sale.

Description: Personal selling is a face-to-face selling technique by which a salesperson uses his or her interpersonal skills to persuade a customer in buying a particular product. The salesperson tries to highlight various features of the product to convince the customer that it will only add value. However, getting a customer to buy a product is not the motive behind personal selling every time. Often companies try to follow this approach with customers to make them aware of a new product.

The company wants to spread awareness about the product for which it adopts a person-to-person approach. This is because selling involves personal touch, a salesperson knows better how to pitch a product to the potential customer. Personal selling can take place through two different channels – through retail and through direct-to- consumer channel. Under the retail channel, a sales person interacts with potential customers who come on their own to enquire about a product. The job of the salesperson is to make sure that he understands the need of the customers and accordingly shows various products that he keeps under that category. Under the direct channel, a salesperson visits potential customers in an attempt to make them aware about a new product that the company is launching or it may have a new offer which the customers may not get from the open market.

Elements Of A Good Pitch

No matter what you are doing in your life - whether it is on a professional level or as a volunteer and whether you are a parent, a teacher, a doctor, a business owner, a politician or any combination of these titles - you are selling something.

In fact, for most people, a day does not go by that you are not selling something to somebody. Money may not always be changing hands, that's true, but when you are trying to convince someone to change a point of view and to come around to your way of thinking, you are selling.

Let's look at a few examples. As a parent, you could be selling the idea of an early bedtime to your child when you yourself are tired. As a student, you may be selling your teacher on why you need more time to take a test. As a neighbor, you may be selling your community the idea that a stop sign is needed at your street corner. As a business owner, you may be selling your new product to a potential investor. As a fundraiser, you may be selling tickets for a charity dinner/auction.

The task of selling and the art of persuading are closely aligned. In his book, "Three Steps to Yes: The Gentle Art of Getting Your Way", Gene Bedell asserts that the ability to sell your ideas, your services and even yourself can impact your life in a way little else can. He says that good salesmanship can make the difference between being in line for a job promotion and being in the unemployment line.

The trouble is many of us equate selling something with being pushy or maybe even with being obnoxious. We think of a salesman as someone working in a used car lot who tries to get you to buy one of his lemons or as a door-to-door magazine peddler who has no intention of ever entering your subscription.

It's time to reimagine the art of salesmanship, and, yes, it is an art. More importantly, it is a skill you can learn and develop. There are five basic strategies to selling anything - goods, services and ideas — and when you have mastered them, you will find you will have radically changed your life for the better. Let's examine five techniques to get someone to say "yes" to whatever you are offering.

Know your customer

Effective public speakers take the time to know their audience. Often they will find out key details about the people in the room such as where they are from, their age range and their educational level. Why? They want to tailor their speech to the specific needs of their listeners. A good salesperson must do the same thing. Before you make an appointment or attend that crucial meeting, find out what you can about the company or the person to whom you are targeting your product or service. The Internet is a great place to start. Check out social media sites such as LinkedIn and Facebook and visit any pertinent websites and blogs. Pay attention to customer feedback the company has received.

Dig for specific information on how your goods or services can benefit the company. Be sure to find out if they have something similar in place, and, if they do, be prepared to discuss why your service is better or at least better for them.

Find out all you can about your market. Regardless of how great your product is, no one will know about it, if you do not target the right people. An important part of research should be determining the correct person or team to contact and how best to reach those individuals. In today's world of super-fast communication, don't let your email or phone call be lost in the shuffle because it wasn't targeted correctly.

Conduct your own market research to find out how effective your product or service is. Use that data to attract new customers. Despite all the wealth of technology we have at our fingertips, the best marketing tool is often positive feedback and good word-of-mouth. Invite customers to tell you what they think of your service. Use that positive feedback to attract new customers who have some of the same needs.

No one likes to have his or her time wasted. The more personal you can make your sales message, the better it will be received. Put yourself in your customer's position and ask yourself what you would want to know about your service. Most people want to learn of things that will make their lives easier or better in some way. How can you meet their specific needs?

Don't make a pitch; have a conversation

The reason many people have a negative connotation of selling is because they think of so-called "hard" selling practices that involve an almost scripted sales pitch filled with exclamations and false promises. To get your customers to say, yes, focus on a conversation, not a pitch.

Often a salesperson will walk away from a lost sale, not understanding what went wrong. "I said everything I wanted to say," he might moan. "The client just wasn't listening." The problem with this scenario - and the resulting lost business agreement - is in who should be listening to whom. Aim to listen more than you talk and you will become a more effective communicator.

Sound counter-intuitive? How can you find out your client's needs if you are doing all the talking? How can you get to know what has worked and not worked for a company in the past if you do not listen? How can you establish a rapport and a common sense of understanding if you do let the other person explain his or her service needs?

Let's face it. We all like to talk about ourselves. We all have egos. That's why, if you can turn the tables by asking open-ended questions that get your customers talking about themselves, you will have opened a very important door to winning the sale.

Think about your first major purchase? Let's say it was a car. It's a scary thing buying a new car, and worrying about all the add-on taxes, title, and interest charges. It's easy to panic and think you can't take the plunge. What if instead of worrying about how much commission he was going to make, the car salesperson just looked at you as a person and asked you questions such as "Is this your first car?" or "What are the things you want in a great car?" or "Who will usually be driving with you?"

These types of questions will trigger a conversation. By listening to your responses and asking some appropriate follow-up questions, the salesperson will get to know you as a person, not just as a dollar sign. In return, you will feel more comfortable, more focused on the good things about buying a new car and less focused on payments.

Now this does not mean that you can ignore the price parameters a customer has set. Part of listening to your customers is respecting what he or she has told you about budget constraints. Let's say your client needs a well-made, versatile business suit for an upcoming interview but has a limited budget. If you ignore the budget and only offer high-priced suits, you will lose the sale.

Resist the urge to tell your customers what they need. By carefully crafting a series of questions, you will instead enable your customers to tell you what they need. Try to think of yourself as a problem solver. The problem in this scenario is how to sell this client the best quality suit he or she can afford. By having a conversation, you can give the customer options to make the best decision, which may include buying a better quality suit at a higher price because it will last longer and therefore save more money in the long run.

As a salesperson, don't compete solely on price. Many a company has succeeded without being competitively priced. Concentrate on need and value, and more importantly, aim to give your customers what they need in order to have good experience with your goods or service. Apple or Nike customers do not choose their products because they are the lowest-price in the market, for example. They choose them because they feel they deliver the experience they want.

If you watch videos of Steve Jobs talking at past Apple product launches, you will realize he stressed customer experience over technology. At the iPhone launch, for example, he didn't say much about the speed of the iPhone's processor or its screen resolution. He did emphasize, however, how easy it is to carry one device as both your music player and your phone. He also discussed the way the device looks, realizing that his customers appreciate the simple, sleek style of Apple products. Remember your customers also care about how your service or product is going to fit into their lives.

Know your product

It's hard to get someone excited about what you are selling if you are not excited about it yourself. Know your product or service inside out and backwards and forwards before you make a sales call. Anticipate questions and be ready with concrete, meaningful answers.

In addition to any pertinent facts and figures, share examples of how your service has helped other people and companies like theirs. The secret is to talk about your product or your service in a way that draws in clients so that they want to be part of what you offer. A good way to achieve this is through the power of storytelling.

Share real life examples of how what you are selling has changed people's lives. Maybe the story of how your company started is inspirational. An example of powerful business storytelling is the founding of TOMS shoes. In his book, Start Something That Matters, Blake Mycoskie explains how a trip to Argentina in 2006 gave him the idea for a business model of helping a person in need with every product purchased. While he started with shoes, Mycoskie's "One for One" program has branched out into eyewear and, most recently, coffee.

People like to hear about personal stories, even if you are selling something that would seem impersonal. "Before and after" stories can be powerful sales tools. Link data with emotion whenever you can. Talk about how using your product makes lives less stressful, more fun or more meaningful. It's hard to say "no" to something inspirational.

Ninety-five percent of what's sold in the world isn't an end unto itself, it's a means to an end. Nobody wants to buy computers; what they want is the ability to transfer information more quickly and accurately so groups can work together better, so they can put products out to market faster, so they can capture more market share. What does the client want to achieve? When you ask that question it changes everything. A key part of knowing your product is to know your competition. Your goal is not to bash your competition but to use what they do to fuel your own success. When asked about his competitors, Bill Gates once said that competition from Google, Apple or even free software helps keep Microsoft on its toes. How can you learn more about what your competitors are up to? Here are a few ideas:

· Shop their services as a customer
· Visit their website and online profiles
· Read and listen to their customers' feedback
· Analyze their advertising and marketing plans

Be prepared for the unexpected

One of the reasons Global Positioning Systems (GPS) have become a problem for drivers rather than a help is because they are not programmed to deal with the unexpected. A GPS may not be programmed for the latest road work delays or for a resulting detour. A GPS does not take into consideration the impact of weather on the time it takes to get somewhere or the safety of the road under extreme circumstances.

Even if you have GPS, it's wise to check the current map and current road conditions before your trip so that you will successfully get to your destination. It is the same with sales. Effective salespeople are confident in their ability to make the sale, but they are humble enough to know that they need to have a back-up plan.

Selling is the practical application of psychology in a business context, according to Brian Tracy, author of The Psychology of Selling. All salespeople encounter objections. Tracy advises that an effective seller interprets objections as questions. Here's an example: If a client says, "The cost of this not is in my budget." Think of it as the question, "How can I afford this?"

If a customer says, "I don't see the use of this product for our firm." Think, "Would you explain to me how this product will help me?" In other words, you can offer counters to objections by offering clear, concise information in response. "Obstacles are necessary for success because in selling, as in all careers of importance, victory comes only after many struggles and countless defeats," writes Og Mandino in his book The Greatest Salesman in the World.

A common roadblock to a sale is the potential customer saying, "I am not the person who has the authority to make this decision." Once again, preparation and a little bit of psychology can get you over this hurdle. Instead of letting this statement back you into a corner, think of it as an opportunity.

Ask the individual who is the best person to contact and if you can count on his or her recommendation for the decision. If the response is ambiguous or negative, use it as an opportunity to offer more information that will be of value to the client.

Follow up

Critical sales can be lost when the salesperson neglects to follow up after the initial sales call. If the meeting ended without a firm commitment all is not lost. You can make yourself stand out by sending a thank you note for the appointment. Did your customer ask for more information? Send it to them. Did someone help you get that appointment in the first place? Thank that individual as well.

With this philosophy in mind, don't just sit there hoping for the sale. Do something original to make it happen. When you communicate your product or ideas effectively, you will persuade others to think as you do. The best way to sell something is to give enough information so that the product or service sells itself or, more accurately, that the customer talks himself into buying it. People don't belive what you tell them. They rarely believe what you show them. They often believe what their friends tell them. They always believe what they tell themselves.

5

Chapter Five

Buyers Are Liars — If They Are Lying They Are Buying

Many small business owners don't have a dedicated sales team and take on the role of sales themselves. This may work out well if the small business owner has a sales background, but what if he has not been trained in sales, and doesn't have a solid grasp on the finer points of selling?

In this case, the small business owner must take time to learn the skill and create a sales plan to guide the process. Often the key is understanding what is stopping a potential client from making a decision in your favor. Once you know why he is hesitating, you can reply directly to that specific objection. You may hear these sales objections during the selling process; learn how you can overcome each objection.

Price Objection

"Your services cost too much. I can get the 'same' service from someone cheaper."

If a client already has the lowest price they believe they can get, you need to help them justify the difference in cost. One of the key ideas here is to know your competition. Know the reliability ratings and review the statistics for the competition's services to help you establish superiority.

Make sure you focus on the unique value of your products and services that the client won't be able to get from any other provider. If your competitor's services or product are good enough you can't overcome objections with value, then there needs to be some analysis conducted to work on the quality of the products or services.

Complacency Objection

"I'm okay with the way things work right now."

When complacency is the culprit, you can try to use just a touch of fear to get the client to see why he needs to start thinking about making changes. Share some research about the competition and some of the changes they have made in their businesses. There is often nothing like a look at what the competition is doing that someone isn't to motivate action.

Fear of Change Objection

"We've been doing things this way for 15 years. Too much can go wrong."

Often related to complacency, a fear of change can make the decision-making process a difficult one for many business owners. One way to overcome this objection is to demonstrate past examples of change and how it was positive. For example, show the client a list of different ways the industry has changed over the past 10 to 15 years, and how the potential customer can adapt to those changes. This can help them be less fearful and more confident about changing things up.

Cost is a big driver against change. Most of the time resistance to change has to do with the costs of changing the methods or equipment in their workplace. Work with the prospect to find ways to make it less of a concern by demonstrating ways to mitigate or cut the costs.

Trust Objection

"It seems like you know what you are doing, but how do I know you really have the necessary experience to do this?"

Trust is something that takes time to build, so if it's a hurdle for your potential client, you need to be honest and consistent across the board to overcome the objection. Be forthcoming with information and share testimonials, case studies and references that will take away some of the uncertainty and give the client confidence in your ability to get the job done.

Family Connections and Promises Objection

"I told my brother's friend's wife I'd use her company for my next project."

Sometimes there's not much you can do to usurp a family connection, but you can get yourself in the position to be the next in line. If this is an objection you're hearing from a potential client, think a few steps ahead and show the client how the services you will provide are better than the family connection. If you can demonstrate that you are saving them both money, you may convince them to switch.

External Input Objection

"I need to run this by my wife/business partner/mentor before I do anything else."

This can often be a positive outcome, assuming the client is truly consulting with others and not just using it as an excuse. One way to make sure it doesn't end up as a deal-ending sales objection is to attempt to stay in the process. Try suggesting a joint sales meeting between the client and their counterpart(s) in order to answer any questions and help facilitate the decision.

Timing Objection

"It's too much for me to take on right now; I'm too busy; call me again in six months."

If time management or lack of time is an issue for the client at this time, chances are it will still be an issue in six months or a year. To overcome this objection, you need to make the decision to use your product or service an easy one for the client.

See if you can find out what is keeping the client so busy. if the client doesn't have time to make decisions, you may have identified a need. Demonstrate how your services can create more time for them. If this is simply a case of disinterest, schedule a call for three months from that day.

Knowledge is the Power of Sales

Keep in mind that your potential clients may have more than one objection so it's important to be able to identify each one as you see it occur. Once you know what is stopping the sales process, you can arm yourself with the right arguments that will tip the scale in your favor. If you know your market and your prospects, you stand a better chance of making sales with them. The key concept behind all these methods is knowledge. If you have done your research and homework and studied the competition, you will be able to overcome all of a prospect's objections. Their indifference and fears will be overcome and satisfied. It's time to close on the client.

Common Sales Objections and the Responses to Overcome Them

Sales objections are quite common in retail, especially for merchants who are selling high-ticket items such as furniture or electronics. Usually, these objections come from customers who are unsure, uninterested or aren't ready to buy. And while it would be wise to respect shoppers' choice to hold off on a purchase, in some cases, you might be able to nudge them in the right direction or actually close the sale.

In this post, we'll be tackling some of the most common objections retailers can encounter when selling to customers. Go through them and see if you can apply them in your business. Before anything else: Read customers and don't be pushy! While the tips below should give you some ideas on how to respond to customer objections, it's important that you first read each shopper and determine the right course of action. For instance, if a shopper is in "just looking around" mode, then it's probably best not to go for the hard sell. There's no "one size fits" all approach for every customer, so don't apply these tips blindly, and don't be pushy or dishonest. That said, let's dive into the objections below and discuss how you can surpass them:

Objection #1: "It's too expensive."

Pricing is probably the most common objection that you'll encounter. And in this case, you'll first have to identify why the customer is concerned about the cost. Is it because the product is really out of their budget, or are they having trouble seeing the value of the item? Is it because they think can purchase it for less elsewhere? Whatever the case may be, figure it out prior to launching your spiel.

If shoppers feel that the item is above their budget, perhaps you can talk about how the product can save them money in the long run. Will it lower their energy bill? Will it "pay for itself" in the long term? If it's a matter of getting the customer to see the value in a product, then you'll need to come up with specific benefits that would justify the cost for the shopper. Before getting into this, you first need to determine why the shopper is looking at a product, as well as how and where they are planning to use the product.

Here's a real-life example: While shopping for a new bed and mattress a while back, the associate I was dealing with asked what brought me to the store and inquired about my bedroom habits. So I explained my routines to her and this helped us narrow down the options. One of the products she recommended was a bed that offered an adjustable base, allowing the user to sit up or recline easily. It was more expensive than other options, but the sales associate was able to justify the cost by saying that an adjustable base would be perfect for someone like me who often uses a laptop in bed. (I happened to mention that I'm always typing away on my computer even in the bedroom.)

Be pointing this out—and demonstrating how the adjustable base oper-ated—she was able to alleviate my concerns about the product's price tag. The good thing about her approach was that she didn't come off as pushy. She didn't try to pressure me into buying the product, and she tailored her recommendation to my specific needs. As a result, I genuinely appreciated her suggestion and ended up completing the purchase. (And yes, I use the bed's feature all the time.)

Objection #2: "Isn't this cheaper online?"

If you're dealing with shoppers who think they can buy the same product for a lower price online (or who are already price checking with their phone), then you can bring up the "hidden costs" that come with Internet purchases. Michael Patrick, founder and president of the retail training company, MOHR Retail, states that retailers can bring up the fact that consumers don't have to pay or wait for shipping.

Merchants can also emphasize that buying the product in person means they know exactly what they're getting and can avoid the hassle of having to return an item because it doesn't meet their expectations. "Often the customer is not thinking about these 'hidden costs,' Patrick adds. "And the fact is, loyalty doesn't come from the lowest price. It comes from salespeople who are authentic and trusted and who demonstrate that they're looking out for the customer."

Objection #3: I need to consult with my significant other first."

If the shopper needs the approval of a parent, significant other, or boss before making a purchase, give thought to the concerns or objections of the third party and then address them with the shopper while you the shopper is still with you. Encourage the customer to bring the third-party to the store so you can speak to them directly, determine the concerns, and close the sale. In some cases trying to get the third party on the phone may help, but doing so might give the appearance of being pushy or that you are trying to rush the customer into making a decision.

Again, the best way to deal with objections is to ask questions, assess the situation (i.e. do they really need to consult with a third party or are they just using this as an excuse?), and react accordingly.

Objection #4: "I've had a bad experience with this product or brand in the past."

First, sympathize and apologize for the inconvenience or problems that your shopper has encountered. Empathize with the customer instead of being on the defensive immediately.

Then second, have the customer explain the issue to you. If it's an issue that you're already aware of, you should have the knowledge or response to address their concerns. For example, you can say that the issue has been fixed in the product's latest model or recommend another brand that doesn't cause the issue. It's also important to reassure the customer that they won't have a similar problem again. Demonstrate that their issues have indeed been addressed and throw in a guarantee to further alleviate any concerns.

Objection #5: "I need to think about it."

When you encounter the "I need to think about it" objection, don't make things uncomfortable by trying to dissuade the customer or rushing the sale. Instead, accept their response by saying "I understand" or "No problem" to put the customer at ease. Depending on how they respond, you may be able to grab a chance to a) address underlying concerns; or b) give them a bit of nudge in the right direction.

You will have to play it by ear to figure out the right approach. Addressing underlying concerns can be done by first determining why they need to think about it. Is it an issue with the price? Are they wary of encountering problems with the product? Whatever the reason is, figure it out and address it accordingly.

On the other hand, if you already know the reason why the customer needs to give a purchase more thought, and you did your alleviate any concerns, then you should give the customer more time to consider the decision. Perhaps you can make the choice easier by instilling a sense of urgency. For example, you can say something like "Just a reminder, our sale ends next week," or something similar.

Objection #6 – I'm happy with what I have right now

Resistance to change often brings up this particular sales objection. By nature, human beings like being in their comfort zone so selling them a product outside of their comfort zone can bring up barriers to the sale.

There are a number of ways to overcome this. First is to show the customer how much better life could be with the new product. Determine the shortcomings of the brand or product they are currently using and talk about how your merchandise can address those issues. For example, if you're selling a pair of Bluetooth headphones, you could talk about how convenient they are and how people who try them never want to come back to using headphones with chords.

Another thing you might do is eliminate risk by allowing a customer to try a product before buying. The lingerie retailer, Third Love, does this well. They have a program that allows its customers to try a bra for 30 days. The shopper just needs to pay for shipping. Once they have the product, they can "wear it, wash it, live in the bra for 30 days." If they love it, they can keep the bra and they'll be charged $68. If the customer is not happy with the merchandise, they can return the item before the 30-day deadline.

Giving out or selling samples and travel sizes can also do the trick. Consider doing the same. If you're dealing with a customer who's not ready to go "all in," sell or offer a sample product so they can try it with little or no risk.

More tips on identifying and handling sales objections

While this is a good starting point to identifying sales objections, there's no substitute for actually speaking to your customers or associates. Jean 'JP' Parker, the VP at Partnerships at Myagi, an education and communication platform for retailers and brands, says that retailers should tap into the knowledge for their front-line teams. It's also important to do it frequently, so customer situations are still fresh in the minds of your managers and associates.

6

Chapter Six

Closing The Front Door

In a perfect world, all your prospects would love you starting your pitch the moment they shook your hand — and then they'd eagerly sign on the dotted line. Unfortunately, deals are almost never that easy to win. It can seem nearly impossible to close when you're dealing with tough customers who make everything more difficult than it needs to be. If clients try to push you around, or they waffle indefinitely over their next steps, deals can drag on for weeks on end. And, chances are, these interactions won't even end in a sale.

How to Close a Sale: 7 Closing Techniues & Why They Work

Closing is a make-or-break moment in sales. Choosing the right phrases to seal a sales deal is crucial. And this moment is likely the final verdict determining whether or not your efforts will amount to anything at all. You're not the only salesperson who feels apprehensive about the close. However, without that feeling of risk, successfully closing a sale wouldn't be so thrilling — which drives salespeople to continuously strive for more.

Because sales professionals are expected to generate the best possible win rates for their effort, a large number of closing sales techniques have been developed over the years. Follows are a few proven closing techniques, and why they are so effective:

- Now or Never Closes
- Summary Closes
- Sharp Angle Closes
- Question Closes
- Assumptive Closes
- Takeaway Closes
- Soft Closes

Traditional Sales Closing Techniues

Traditional sales closing techniques usually employ some psychological tricks designed to give that final nudge. Here are two of the most common.

Now or Never Closes

This is where salespeople make an offer that includes a special benefit that prompts immediate purchase. For example:

- "This is the last one at this price."
- "We've got a 20% discount just for customers who sign up today."
- "If you commit to buy now, I can fast track you to the front of the implementation queue."

This technique works because it creates a sense of urgency and can help overcome inertia when a prospect wants to buy— but for some reason is not pulling the trigger. Of course, you should always establish value before offering a discount or promotion.

Summary Closes

Salespeople who use this closing technique reiterate the items the customer is considering purchasing (stressing the value and benefits) in an effort to get the prospect to sign.

For example:

"So we have the Centrifab washing machine with brushless motor, the 10-year comprehensive guarantee and our free delivery and installation service. When would be a good time to deliver?"

By summarizing previously agreed-upon points into one impressive package, you're helping prospects visualize what they are truly getting out of the deal.

Sharp Angle Closes

Prospects often ask for price reductions or add-ons because they know they have the upper hand — and they also know you expect it. If you have approval from your sales manager to do so, try the sharp angle close technique to catch these prospects by surprise.When they ask, "Could you add on a few extra hours of onboarding at a discounted rate?" reply, "Sure. But if I do that for you, will you sign the contract today?" It's likely they won't be expecting this response — first, because you agreed to their request, and second, because you've proposed closing today.

Modern Sales Closing Techniques

These canned closing techniques probably seem a little oldfashioned. Perhaps they strike you as a little too "salesy," particularly in light of the rise of inbound sales. In particular, the closing itself needs to encompass any and all incremental agreements you secure throughout a sales process — not just the moment of final purchase. In a sales engagement, reps should endeavor to:

- Discover the customer's needs
- Effectively communicate how specific products or services offer an affordable and satisfactory solution to meet their needs.

If these two requirements are properly achieved, then there should be no barrier to closure. The closing question can be asked directly at that point.

Quick reminder:

Be sure to track all of the information you collect at this stage in a free CRM. The data might not seem immediately useful,but keeping track of objections from a prospect can help you organizationally improve and close more deals in the longrun.

Question Closes

To achieve these two foundational goals, it's imperative that reps ask prospects probing questions. Effective salespeople focus on closing a sale as soon as a conversation with a prospect begins. Through a series of questions, they develop desire in the client and eliminate every objection to purchase.One can even close the sale in the form of a question, which allows the rep to address outstanding objections while gaining a commitment at the same time. For example:

"In your opinion, does what I am offering solve your problem?"

The question allows you to discover whether the prospect is sold on your product while keeping the doors open for further selling. If the answer is 'no', it remains their opinion (not yet the truth), thereby allowing you to further sell... If the answer is 'yes,' then signing on the dotted line is the next step. Here's another question close:

"Is there any reason why we can't proceed with the shipment?"

This question asks either for closure or more information as to why the customer isn't quite ready. It's a win-win.

Assumptive Closes

This closing technique draws on the power of positive thinking. If you believe from the first piece of email outreach you will close this deal, it can have an incredible effect on the rest of the sales process.

What's important here is to closely monitor your prospect's interest, engagement, and objections throughout. After a call or meeting, ask, "Did this presentation align with your expectations?" If you've just provided them with new information about your product or service, ask, "Does this sound like something that would be valuable to your company? Does this meet a specific need or pain point?" By keeping your ear to the ground — and assuming good intent from the start — you will bring an authority and direction to your sales process that wouldn't be there otherwise.

Take Away Closes

If you have kids you've most likely noticed that if you take a toy away from a child, they will want that toy more than ever. Use this similar psychological practice on your prospects.

If they're balking on price, remove a feature or service and present the discounted offer to them. It's likely, they'll be thinking about the part you removed rather than the discounted price.

Soft Closes

The soft close is a way to show your prospect the benefit of your product and then ask a low-impact question to ascertain whether the prospect is open to learning more.

For example:

"If I could reduce widget maintenance by 25% and increase widget productivity by 15%, would you be interested in learning more?"

You have clearly stated the benefits without making any demands or sudden requests. If the example above still seems too direct, you could ask, "If I told you I could reduce widget maintenance by 25% and increase widget productivity by 15%, would that align with your company goals?"

This removes their need to immediately commit to you in the slightest, and gives you more time to learn about their business needs. Being skilled at closing is arguably one of the most important techniques a salesperson can master. Find a mentor or fellow salesperson who excels at it and learn from them.

Keys to Closing Tough Customers in Sales

While you can't control prospects' attitudes, you can control your responses. You can take productive steps to increase your chances of closing the sale — even when you're dealing with the worst customers imaginable. With these six keys to closing tough customers in sales, you will be more prepared to deal with bullies, noncommittal prospects, and just plain difficult people. Implement them now and start to crush your competition in sales.

- Don't react or display anxiety

- Stay firm
- When necessary, mirror their response
- Probe into their challenges
- Understand their top priorities
- Secure true buy-in
- Maintain conversational control
- Never try to prove your dominance
- Remember, it's not personal

Show that you're unfazed

If difficult prospects sense you are uncomfortable or nervous, they will be even more likely to try to take advantage of you. Resist the urge to speed up the sales meeting or alter your approach in response to a tough customer's poor attitude. Instead, show that you are unfazed by staying on message (sticking to your script) — even if you are being pressured by the customer to hurry things along.

Be firm at all times

It's natural to feel frustrated when a prospect is giving you a difficult time — but frustration will only waste your opportunity. After all the prospect may be a bully, but he more than likely he still needs what you're selling. Don't take anything personally, and commit to standing your ground. Keep your emotions in check and stay on track with your regular approach to closing sales.

When in doubt, match the prospect

Occasionally the best way to keep a bully inline is to match them. Rise to their tone, pace, and strength, and you may be surprised to find the bully backing down in response. By matching that type of personality, you're more likely to win their respect and hold their attention.

Get prospects talking about their challenges

Difficult prospects have a million different things on their minds. They simply don't want to listen to you. Instead of forcing them to listen to what you want to say, try to get the difficult customer to talk about themselves and challenges confronting them. With this approach, you can tap into their emotional side and break through the animosity. For prospects who are hesitant to commit, getting them to talk about their key challenges can help you gauge how much of a priority solving their problem(s) truly is.

Understand prospects' top objectives

Ask your prospects which goals they most want to accomplish in the short term. Try asking, "What are your top priorities in the next 6, 12, or 18 months?" By aligning your solution with those objectives, you can create greater urgency for even the most noncommittal clients.

Get real commitment

Before you get to your proposal, find out how serious the prospect is about solving the challenges and objectives they have discussed with you. Instead of asking if the customer is committed to buying your product or service, try asking, "George, are you committed to doing something about this right now?" By holding your prospect's feet to the fire, you'll be able to gauge whether or not the prospect is ready to commit to what you have to offer.

Maintain conversational control

When dealing with difficult prospects (or their colleagues), it's not uncommon for that person to hijack the conversation. This looks like someone pursuing irrelevant tangents, steering the conversation in different directions, and speaking over you. It's important for the salesperson to maintain control over the conversation at all times. If you notice things getting out of hand, don't hesitate to politely interrupt with, "Excuse me, I'd be happy to speak to this point more after the presentation, but I'd like to respect everyone's time by keeping to our agenda by staying on track." This should allow you to wrangle the conversation back to you and your prospect's collective goals.

Never try to prove your dominance

"Did you know …," "Actually," and "No offense" are all statements used to prove dominance. They are missteps in a sales conversation and power moves that won't serve you well when dealing with the difficult prospect. It's natural to want to position yourself as an authority figure in dealings with tough customers — but do this by sharing information objectively and asking for your prospect's perspective.

For example, instead of saying, "Did you know industry experts predict widget production will triple in the next four years?", try, "I've heard widget production is expected to triple in the next four years. Will this affect your business at all?"

In the first example, you're trying to one-up your customer with industry intel they don't know. In the second example, you've presented them with a fact, and asked for them to weigh in.

Remember, it's not personal

Tough customers are just part of the game of sales. They'll never go away, but it's important not to take their behavior too seriously. Always be respectful in meetings, but if things get out of hand leave it at the office. It's not a reflection on you and is likely the sign of personal struggles the prospect is facing. Go home, have dinner, chat with a friend, and unwind so you can come back tomorrow fully charged. Tough customers are never fun — but they can still be profitable. With a game plan in place, you'll be far less likely to fold under pressure or take difficult selling situations personally.

7

Chapter Seven

Be On A First Name Basis

Whether you're in a niche industry or you have thousands of other competitors, maintaining an active relationship with your customers is crucial to business growth. More often than not we see companies pouring their time, energy and money into acquiring new customers but they're missing out on the biggest market of all – their current customers. After all, statistics speak for themselves: customer acquisition costs seven times more than customer retention and 81% of customers are more likely to give repeat business simply because they were provided good service. Convinced? Here are some ways that you can nurture your customer relationship to build trust and turn them into lifelong fans.

Be Intentional

It begins with a mindset. This is often one of the biggest obstacles to cross in order to effectively nurture your current customer relationships. You have to intentionally seek and plan for opportunities to engage. Garter Group in "Leading on the Edge of Chaos" found that companies that prioritized customer relationships saw 60% high profits than their competitors. So you must plan for it to be successful lotherwise it's easy to get caught up in other day-to-day, business activities.

Be Attentive

Each of us has some level of interaction with our clients, whether it's through face-to-face meetings, emails, questionnaires, or just sign up information. Information is key to establishing strategic, stronger relationships with your customers. To help you with this process, document everything you know about each of your customers and have it easily accessible in order to not only tailor your communication and services to them, but also so you can know how to better market to them in future interactions.

Give Them First Looks

People love to be the first to know about new and exciting changes that could affect them as a consumer. One way to build consumer loyalty is to give them a firstlook into new products, services, deals, etc. This not only creates a stronger sense of belonging and loyalty within your customer base, but it also is a great way to start some buzz around your products, services and/or brand.

Get Feedback

Your greatest asset are your customers, so why not utilize them to improve your organization, products or services while developing stronger relationship with them? Asking for feedback is one of the best ways to do this. People want to be heard and know that they are actually being heard. Asking current customers about their experiences, thoughts and suggestions, opens the door for future interactions with them and even may provide an emotional tie. Give them a specific, easy way to communicate their thoughts, either through email, a survey, a website form, social media, or some other collection platform to help push them past any hesitation.

Stay Engaged

Finally, the biggest mistake we can make as an organization after someone purchases our product, uses our services or completes the active customer lifecycle, is to stop communicating with them. The goal should be to retain those customers for future business, to use as referrals or simply just for them to advertise you by word-of-mouth. After all, studies have found that a 5% increase in customer retention increases profits up to 125%. To put develop a viable plan of communication, create checkpoints during a customer lifecycle and after to purposefully engage with your customers in some way.

Check-in from time to time in a personal way (even if it looks automated), either with new offers, company updates or a simple "how's it going" email. Developing stronger relationships with your client base doesn't have to be overcomplicated. It's more about being intentional about seeking out opportunities to engage with them which will, in turn, help them develop a loyalty to you and your brand.

8

Conclusion

We have come to the end of this book. You must have learned that in persuading anyone of anything, especially in persuading a prospect to hand over cash for goods and or services, you have to be authentic. Some motivators tell you to get excited about your company and your product whether you feel it or not – jump up and down before a presentation, listen to loud music, read an inspirational quote, recite affirmations. This is supposed to improve your appeal. I can tell you if you just want to make your eyes sparkle it takes a lot less energy to pull three hairs out of your nose. If you don't already feel it, no amount of fakery will get you warmed up.

- You need to feel good about sales without needing to pump yourself up.
- You need to feel good about the product or service you're selling without needing to re-read the brochure.
- You need to feel good about the company you represent without needing to be re-inducted every day. Fix your feelings or flee!

- You see those people in government offices stumbling around like clock-work crash dummies day in and day out?
- See those sales people gossiping and texting?

- See those trade reps parked under a tree for three hours?
- See that salesperson so reluctant every day to get out of bed and face the job?

None of them feel good about where they work, who manages them, what they sell or to whom they sell. They stay at what they do because they need the money. There's no honor in their work, no joy, no purpose because there is no feeling for what they do. They are selling their souls for a few perishable coins. There is real joy in meaningful work, and none in forced labor.

So use your feelings

Let's say you love your product, love your company, love your boss, and even love your customers (bless you!) Most sales people are in this position. So why, oh why, Oh WHY don't you let your feelings flow? Why do you rave on about facts and specifications and dimensions and weight per square foot poundal and ergonomic capacities per megalitre and reputational comparisons and ROI per micro-cent and why don't you SHUT UP and ask a question to see if being so boring is getting through? Yes, eventually the facts and figures will appeal to someone I suppose, but what the customer eventually buys is your feeling, your joy, yourconfidence, your ideas, your love. Let it loose.

Buying decisions are always the result of a change in the customer's emotional state. While information may help change that emotional state, it's the emotion that's important,not the information. All buying decisions stem from the interplay of the following six emotions:

- Greed: "If I make a decision now, I will be rewarded."
- Fear: "If I don't make a decision now, I'm toast."
- Altruism: "If I make a decision now, I will help others."
- Envy: "If I don't make a decision now, my competition will win."
- Pride: "If I make a decision now, I will look smart."
- Shame: "If I don't make a decision now, I will look stupid."

Every successful sales approach either created or augmented one or more of these emotional states. When enough of these emotions are present inside the buyer's emotional state, a buying decision becomes inevitable.

Understand Your Customer's Beliefs. However, these changes in emotional state can only be accomplished when the sales approach takes into account the customer's belief system. It is this belief system that determines how each emotion play out.

For example, if a potential buyer sees IBM as her main competition, the "fear" and "envy" emotions will be vivid if the sales approach emphasizes competing with IBM. (In the high-tech world, this is called "waving the blue flag of death.")

By contrast, if the potential buyer is an executive at IBM, she might be more afraid (and also a tiny bit envious) of competition from an unidentified upstart firm with the potential to disrupt a cash cow product. Similarly, a sales message that "this is a green product that saves the environment" might score high on the "altruism" scale of some crunchy-granola executive in Seattle, but fall dead flat when presented to a decision maker who is politically conservative.

In other words, if you're going to create emotions that drive decision-making, you need to know, not just the audience's current emotional state, but also the beliefs that are using to evaluate the emotional weight of anything that you might present to them.

And that means research. The more thoroughly you research your audience, the more likely you'll be to understand their current state and the better you will marshal emotions to change that state.

What You Need to Learn

It is in this context that information finally comes into play. The emotional change you're seeking in your customer will probably result from the expression of new information and the reframing of old information.

Remember, though, that it is not the information itself that is important, but the emotional effect that the information has on your audience. This is an essential distinction.

For example, suppose you're trying to sell an inventory control system to a high-tech firm. Your research indicates that the company has been dinged by investors for having high inventories, and its main competitor has just implemented a "just in time" inventory system. That's just information. What's really important is the emotional effect that those two facts will have when juxtaposed with one another-based on the prospect's likely belief system.

Similarly, let's suppose your research also reveals that the prospect's CIO was just replaced and the new CIO was promoted from the ranks. What is important in this case is that the new CIO may lack confidence and is probably be risk-averse.

www.ingramcontent.com/pod-product-compliance
Lightning Source LLC
Chambersburg PA
CBHW021500210526
45463CB00002B/824